THE HAMBLE RIVER
and much about Old Bursledon

SUSANNAH RITCHIE

GW00492775

REVISED EDITION

ACKNOWLEDGEMENTS

So many people contributed photographs and their
memories to the two previous printings of
THE HAMBLE RIVER, and I would again thank
them for their continued interest in this third
edition. Sadly some friends are no longer with us,
but for the photographs this time I would like to
mention Jonathan Eastland of Ajax Photos,
Colin Bowler, the Friends of Bursledon Windmill,
YMCA Fairthorne Manor,
Harold Fay, Mrs. R.J. Gillman, Terry Madden,
Capt. P.G. Mitchell, R.N., Mrs. P. Newenham,
Peter Page, and Miss Daphne Williamson.

Published by Milestone Publications of
62 Murray Road, Horndean, Hampshire in 1984. Reprinted 1988.

Third edition published by

TANDEM DESIGN
of Eastgate Street, Southampton. 1996.

ISBN 0 9528238 0 2

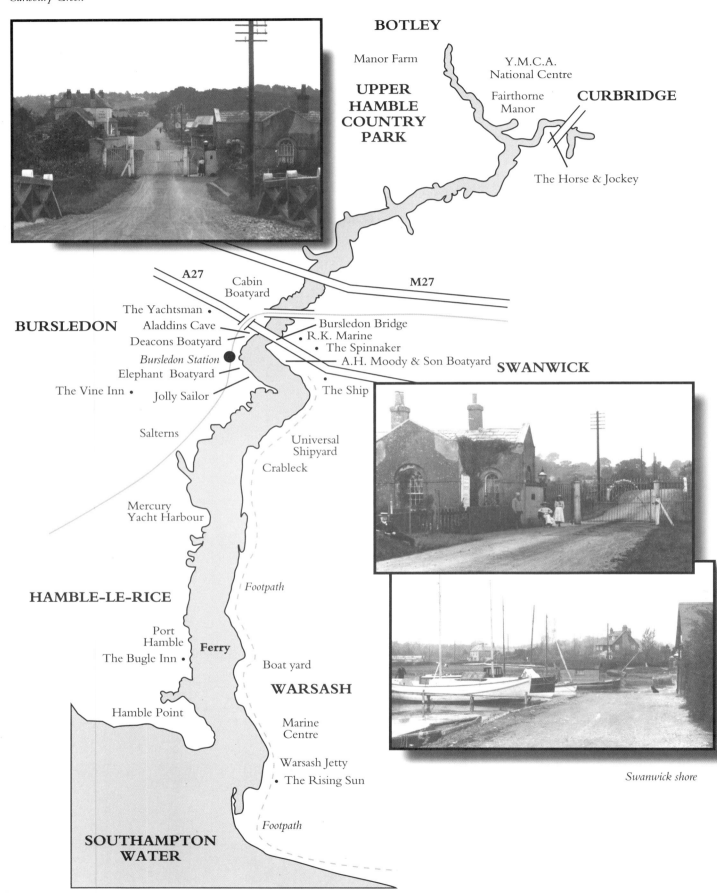

From Bursledon toll bridge looking towards Sarisbury Green

BOTLEY

Manor Farm

Y.M.C.A.
National Centre

UPPER
HAMBLE
COUNTRY
PARK

Fairthorne
Manor

CURBRIDGE

The Horse & Jockey

A27

Cabin
Boatyard

M27

The Yachtsman •

BURSLEDON

Aladdins Cave

Deacons Boatyard

Bursledon Station ●

Elephant Boatyard

The Vine Inn •

Jolly Sailor

Bursledon Bridge

• R.K. Marine

• The Spinnaker

A.H. Moody & Son Boatyard

SWANWICK

• The Ship

Salterns

Universal
Shipyard

Crableck

Mercury
Yacht Harbour

Footpath

HAMBLE-LE-RICE

Port
Hamble

Ferry

The Bugle Inn •

Boat yard

WARSASH

Hamble Point

Marine
Centre

Warsash Jetty

• The Rising Sun

Swanwick shore

Footpath

SOUTHAMPTON
WATER

Hamble River at Swanwick (1950)

The Hamble River flows into Southampton Water at its South Eastern edge, nearly opposite Calshot. To the North are its neighbours the Itchen which emerges where the cross-Channel ferries berth, and the Test at the upper end of the Docks.

The Hamble, known to yachtsmen the world over, is the most popular yachting harbour on the South Coast, and is crowded to capacity, with its forest of masts on moorings and in the various marinas.

Into this estuary, long ago, came parties of Jutes and Saxons on their way to good land up-country where they could settle, and also came the longboats of the Danes, who fought a battle with King Alfred's ships in the Solent in the year 897, and lost, which discouraged their raids for a while. The Venerable Bede wrote of it as the 'Homelea' - flowing from the land of the Jutes. But evidence of earlier people has been found near the mouth of the river. When a private golf course was being constructed in 1930 at Hook Park on the east bank, for Sir Warden Chilcott, there were found the sites and 'briquetage' where salt had been evaporated. These were inspected by the late Mr. C.F. Fox of Old Bursledon (a member of the Hampshire Field Club & Archeological Society) and the few pieces of domestic pottery found were dated by Mr. Christopher Hawkes, F.S.A. of the British Museum, as from the 1st Century B.C. to the 1st Century A.D. with some run-on into mid Roman. It was considered that the saltworkers would have imported the domestic pottery, as their own skill did not go beyond making the clay 'briquetage' under which their fires burned - and they presumably needed shallow pans in which the water could be evaporated. It is interesting to speculate on the kind of men they

were who busied themselves on the shore with this primitive extraction of salt - the notes made by Mr. Fox said that the base of one of the struts carried the deep impression of a potter's huge fingerprints!

Bursledon, the main subject of our book has arrived at that name over a period of seven centuries, changing from Brixedone to Brixenden to Bristleden to Bussleton through the centuries - but the original, 'Brixedon', is happily perpetuated in the farm of that name. Forests once lined the banks of the Hamble, and so the sheltered river, and in particular Bursledon, became the site of shipyards from the time of the first 'wooden walls'. The Royal Navy's first man o'war, the St. George, was built at Bursledon and launched on St. George's Day 1338 by King Edward III,but the peak of shipbuilding was the 17th, 18th and early 19th centuries, in the time of the Wyatts, the Ewers and George Parsons.

The area of Bursledon, Netley and Hamble was rather isolated for centuries because it was enclosed by the rivers Itchen and Hamble, a fact which tended to make the agricultural community of these parts rather clannish, with much inter-relationship of a few well known local families.

Anyone wishing to cross the River Hamble had to be rowed across by the ferryman and there was a ford by the site of the present railway bridge at Bursledon, connecting with Blundells Lane. From there the road went to Winchester and beyond. Then, in 1798, the Northam Bridge Company and the Bursledon Bridge Company (many of the directors being common to both companies) built toll bridges across the Itchen and Hamble, so making the communications between Southampton and Portsmouth and all places between so much easier.

Bursledon Old Bridge

In its first year (1800) the toll takings at Bursledon were £126 but in the year 1815 (Battle of Waterloo) the takings increased to £2,148, an all time high, and again in 1915 takings were well into four figures - no doubt the common cause being military traffic! Increasing traffic resulted in the adoption by the Council in 1929 and the building of the present concrete bridge in 1934. The railway was by that time already carried by the iron bridge and of course in the 1970s a third bridge was constructed over the river to carry the motorway.

Approaching by water from the mouth of the Hamble, on the starboard side is the Warsash Marine Centre of Southampton Institute, known to hundreds of seagoing officers as the School of Navigation where they received their training. During the war (1939/45) there was a Naval Base H. M.S. 'Tormentor', here, and Wren crews ferried landing craft to and from the local yards for repairs to be done. In charge of the girls was Miss L.C. Edwards, a very experienced local yachtswoman who, in 1937, had the distinction of being the first of her sex to gain a Yachtmaster's Certificate at Southampton.

On the waterfront is the Rising Sun, and the Harbour Master's fine lighthouse looking tower from whence he has a good view of all passing shipping. The foreshore car park should be avoided on spring tides, when it is safer to use the large park at the rear of the boatyard. There was a lobster pond on the shore in days gone by into which the creatures were tipped from the fishing boats, pending sale. The crab and lobster business was well established at Hamble and Warsash from about 1860 onwards, but by 1920 only four ketches remained in the trade.

The village shopping centre clusters around the Clock Tower which is a relic of the Warsash House estate, which belonged in turn to Lord Stalbridge who kept his beautiful three masted schooner 'Cetonia' on the river, and Mr. George Shenley, who had the steam yacht "Triad". The house was destroyed by fire, and all that remains of it is a dovecot, the thatched cottage which was the dairy, and the huge Warsash Oak which is a protected tree. Around are the modern houses which were built in the old garden.

Shore Road, Warsash

Rising Sun, Warsash 1950

Warsash Yard 1945

Hamble Main Street

Hamble foreshore before 1939

The riverside path leads to the ferry which connects Warsash and Hamble. It has progressed from costing one penny when passengers were rowed across, to 50p now that a motorboat operates. This path could be used from Warsash to Swanwick before the last war, but the embankment was breached, and was not repaired. Afterwards successive councils put off any action, so the gaps grew larger, and so did the sums of money required to repair the damage. The marsh inside the bank became a lagoon at each high tide, which conservationists welcomed because it attracts birdlife – at the same time it is the only good length of the Hamble to which walkers have access and an opportunity to enjoy an unrestricted view of the yachting. Work was started in 1980 on the restoration of the path and was then completed. It is in these seagrass meadows and verges that the name of the village originated – old papers relating to the surrender of Titchfield Abbey in 1537 gave it as Warish Asse Field, because donkeys were turned out to graze along the river bank.

Inland, the Warsash/Hook/Abshot area was sparsely populated and mainly concerned with strawberry growing and market-gardening, but this has now moved into glasshouse production of tomatoes, cucumbers and chrysanthemums, with some interesting developments in hydrophonics –

growing plants in water. The nurseries growing flowering plants have benefited from the increasing number of garden centres which need stocking. Hamble Le Rice, across the river from Warsash, is thought to have derived its official name – which appears on old maps and milestones – from the Norman French 'en le rys' indicating that it stood on a little hill. The ship interest is much in evidence in the church of St. Andrew, with many most interesting memorials. Benedictine monks from the Abbey of Tiron near Chartres, founded a priory here between 1109 and 1128, this being dissolved in 1390 with other French settlements, and the present church was built in the 15th Century by Winchester College – the early Bursledon records of baptisms, marriages and burials being recorded in the Hamble registers.

There is a very long path from the lychgate to the church door, which must be a trial to brides in all their finery, on wet and windy days, since there is no alternative to walking.

There are some notable houses, between the church and the Square is the Old White Hart (1563), the 17th Century Gun House, Copperhill Terrace also facing the Square, and another timber-framed brick-infilled house around which traffic has to edge its way down the main street. Fortunately this is too narrow for any 'heavies'.

Strawberry pickers at farm in Swanwick Lane

Hamble was famous early this century for its involvement with the development of flying and its consequent association with such names as AVRO, Armstrong Whitworth, Folland, Fairey Aviation, Supermarine and the Air Service Training School, and the Gnat and Mosquito planes.

R.A.Calvert, who worked as a draughtsman with many of the aeroplane designers, and, incidentally, was with the Cierva team who invented the helicopter, told a tale that when a prize was offered for the first seaplane in a race around the British Isles, the machines were gathered at Hamble Point. At the time appointed not one of them was ready, but a week later Harry Hawker, an Australian, took off, and after flying all day arrived in Dublin Bay, where he was obliged to give up because of sunstroke...! However, as the other competitors did not get even thus far, he was reckoned to have won.

With Grenada much in the news it is perhaps here relevant to say that Reg Calvert, who was very well known on the Hamble and in latter years had lived on his little yacht in St. George's Harbour at Grenada, was, in 1980, hi-jacked by two men who broke out of jail one night, and he was presumed murdered by them. The yacht turned up, stripped of all her gear and holed, on the shore of St. Lucia. A sad end.

From the bank here at Hamble on can view the procession of the latest and most expensive yachts as they pass in and out of the entrance. John Oakeley, who did so much of the trial sailing with "Lionheart" (Britain's 1980 entry in the Americas Cup), is a local man. Mr. Edward Heath's "Morning Cloud" is based at Hamble, the beautiful three masted "Royalist" has a brief winter spell at the Swanwick Marina, and Mr. Adlard Coles kept his series of famous "Cohoe" yachts in the river when he lived at Bursledon. Mr. Coles was awarded the Yachtsman of the Year Trophy in 1957 when, in "Cohoe III", he won in his class the Fastnet, the Channel Race, the La Rochelle to Benodet, and the Points Championship of the R.O.R.C. All this when he was fifty-five years of age. In 1950 he had won the 3.000 mile Transatlantic Race from Bermuda to Plymouth.

Another Hamble based yachtsman, sadly missed since his sudden death in 1981, is Dave Johnson, with his lovely "Casse Tete" yachts. He had been a well known sailor around the river, and in offshore racing, since his days in the R.A.F. locally when he learned

Hamble Manor

R.A. Calvert and the author

to sail with the Forces team. As well as being an entry in yacht "Casse Tete V" for the Admirals Cup and the Sardinia Cup, he was also a competitor in the 1979 Fastnet Race - the race which will surely be remembered by even those with no particular interest in yacht racing, and which served to change some of the race rules. The competitors met the most terrible storm conditions, and although this race is always regarded as a great test of boats and crews, the fact that fifteen people died and 136 were rescued from twenty-three boats which were abandoned or sunk, spells out the lesson that the sea will periodically assert her strength.

Angus Primrose and Moody 33 'Demon Demo'

Another well known Hamble yachtsman and designer, Angus Primrose, was lost in 1980 in a sudden storm off the coast of America. He had been sailing all his life, and was the designer of a complete range of Moody yachts. The famous Colonel 'Blondie' Hasler paid tribute to him in a service which crowded the parish church at Hamble with his friends. He said that Angus won a yachting magazine competition for a design while he was still at school, and a man who wrote to him about building the yacht was amazed to find that the designer 'who made an appointment to meet him at a pub near the school' was only fourteen years old, The man was so impressed that he went ahead and built the boat, and that was the beginning of the Primrose career. Perhaps as a result of this Angus gave much time and good advice to

youngsters who wrote to him, and always sent carefully studied replies to their problems. He was a kind man, and his death was a great loss to the yachting scene.

In the first decades of yachting on the Hamble River the Southampton Harbour Board had control of the waterway, and they let mooring sites to boat owners and boatyards, who had to supply their own ground tackle, anchors and chains, and maintain this gear. In the nineteen fifties piles were driven into the river bed between the mouth and Bursledon Bridge to accommodate two vessels between each set. The S.H.B. had an interesting method of electing replacement members to the Board when anyone died or retired. All the Waterfrontagers (their official name) had a certain number of votes according to the extent of the property they owned on the banks of the Hamble, Itchen or Southampton Waterfront. Prospective candidates for a seat therefore had to contact all these people and obtain their favour, in writing, under the official Seal of the company - in the case of firms who had a block of votes.

Hamble from river

Before World War II Hamble Hard was a muddy expanse, but the American Army used it, and when they left it was transformed. Now there are places for parking cars and boats, and from here in the summer one can embark on river trips. Overlooking the scene is the restaurant of the Bugle Inn, and at one end the Royal Southern Yacht Club with its magnolia tree. The Royal Air Force Club is at Riverside House, once the home of the Scovell family who owned fishing vessels and a building yard, and the Hamble River Sailing Club members built themselves a wooden club house at first where the ferry crossed to Warsash.

Hamble Regatta takes place in midsummer, and thus spaces out well with the Bursledon, Swanwick and Warsash one which is held in late August or early September. The old idea was that the lateness of this event enabled the local yacht hands to get back from summer cruising, but this no longer applies, there being few paid crew members nowadays. The offshore racing yachts are crewed by keen young men who work in the cities and appear at weekends to take part for love of the sport.

Of course, many local youngsters sail, which would have cheered the heart of a certain Captain Nelson (a connection of the Admiral), who lived in Hamble years ago. Reg Calvert, who was Sea Scout Master in the nineteen twenties, described the wrath and indignation when Captain Nelson was told that a well-wisher had presented the Scouts with a motor boat. "How can they make good sailors with an engine?" demanded the Captain.

Following the 1914/18 War hundreds of ex-Admiralty 70ft. motor launches (Canadian built, of wood), were moored in tiers from just above Hamble village to Swanwick, in the Long Reach, pending sale. The Hamble Sea Scouts were given permission to go aboard and use one of the craft as a meeting place. This offer they gladly accepted but they found that as soon as they had tidied up the decks of a particular boat and installed themselves, the craft was chosen by a new purchaser who came along - largely because it looked so much better of course!
After losing several boats on which they had laboured, they realised what was happening, and left their next choice looking as scruffy as possible on the outside while they cleared it up within.....

There are three marinas at Hamble. Coming into the river the first one is at Hamble Point, alongside the Fairey Marine Yard. Then there is Port Hamble, on the site of the old Luke Brothers Yard, and the third is the Mercury Yacht Haven near the spot at which the Training Ship "Mercury" was moored. (This old ship, known locally as "Noah's Ark", started life in 1818 as H.M.S. "Gannett".) The Mercury Training Ship was founded by a Mr. Hoare in 1885 and was

for some years in the charge of C.B.Fry, the England cricketer. On Sunday afternoons the boys would walk several miles in crocodile formation, although they sounded more like starlings....

In 1979 the school closed, the shore establishment was demolished, and an estate of small houses sprang up. However, the developers had left a riverside walk for the length of the estate, which is good, since there is very limited access on the west bank. On the left of the gate to the church is a memorial to the 'Mercury Boys' who were lost in the two World Wars.

As we take our imaginary craft up the river we pass the entrance to Badnam Creek, once a waterway giving access to the Hungerford Valley where the ironworkers made bolts and fittings for the old naval ships. The coming of the railway blocked off the top of the creek, and in fact altered the whole waterside area around Bursledon Pool. Up to fifty years ago coasters loaded gravel and loam from a jetty at the entrance to Badnam Creek. There is still a good deal of gravel extracted from the land in the Netley / Hamble / Butlocks Heath areas, but it now has to go by lorry.

Here on our starboard side, we are abreast of the Universal Shipyard, inland and up river from which are the well wooded and beautiful sites of three large estates. Sarisbury Court was pulled down sometime after the First World War, having ended its days as a Government Training Centre for ex-Servicemen. Smaller houses have settled down amongst the original trees. Holly Hill belonged to the famous Quinton Hogg (Lord Hailsham), and the first mansion was destroyed by fire, believed to have been caused by the sun's rays striking a magnifying glass. Mr. Hogg had the house rebuilt, but this one too was burnt - at which point he gave up and sold the estate. The present Holly Hill House is an Old Peoples' Home, and for a long time the gardens were a jungle, but someone on the Fareham UDC had the extremely good idea of employing out of work lads to clear the undergrowth, drain and clear the pools and feeder streams, and generally improve the area.

This has been a spectacular success, and it is now a great local amenity, with the water populated by a variety of ducks. It was by no means an easy task as the mud had to be dug out by manual labour, no machinery was used. The gardens were originally designed by Sir Joseph Paxton, and there are some alien rocks at the lower end of the water.

The gardens are entered from the main Sarisbury Green to Warsash road, where signposted "Cemetery and Holly Hill Mansion", or from Holly Hill Lane nearer the river.

Also approached from Sarisbury Green by way of Holly Hill Lane is Universal Shipyard, which is on the east bank of the river in the Long Reach, and alongside it is another gathering of boats at Crableck. The third house is 'Brooklands' which is the large white building by the Swanwick bend of the river. The de Selincourt family owned it for some years. In the spring the bright colours of rhododendrons and azaleas show through the trees which clothe the bank of the river here, and the trees themselves make a beautiful stand, particularly in the spring and autumn, with their varying shades.

The cluster of houses at Swanwick Shore includes the 'Old Ship' (alongside the A27), one nice old thatched cottage, and a row of the smallest imaginable houses tucked in behind Moody's Yard. Some of the more modern buildings have a splendid view down the Long Reach, but are exposed to the full force of southerly gales. The 'Old Ship' (at the time known as 'Oslands') was once the home of Stanley Steele, a great supporter of the 'X' Class, and, considerably earlier than that, of one, Jonathan Southam, a brickmaker and potter. Having rounded the bend in the river, we can alight on the public hard by 'Lands End House'. This house is on

the site of an inn, "The Ship and Launch". Here the crews of the sailing coasters danced to the music of a fiddler who appeared when vessels were due. While the loading and unloading of the barges from Botley was in progress, the coasters lay in the deep water channel in the shelter of the bank, and the sailors took advantage of a few days relaxation.

The scene of their revelry was the place at which a stray bomb fell in 1941, killing Eric Humphery, son of the owner of the house, as he walked through the garden.

Sarisbury Court

Lands End House 1910

Cottages at Swanwick shore

From Mr. W.G. Richards' family came the story that sailors who fell overboard and were drowned from the coasters which lay along the Lands End shore, were buried inside the fence by the church lychgate, one them was a Chinese, and in an unmarked grave.

Another item from the past from this source is that before there was any bridge at Bursledon, and before John Ekless had instigated the building of the church at Sarisbury Green, the people of Swanwick went to Bursledon Church by way of the ferry from Swanwick Shore to Lands End Hard. It would be interesting to know how many used this route each Sunday... and how best bonnets survived the crossing in an open boat on wet and windy mornings.

The petition to Parliament in the 18th century for a bridge to be built says;

From the violence of the winds and sea the passage over the said river by the said ferry is often dangerous and frequently totally prevented; by reason whereof any communication between the said places (Bursledon and Swanwick) by means of the said ferry becomes impracticable, and inconvenience and loss are thereby incurred.

Here, on our right as we stroll up the road, is the house now known as "Parsons Plot" – this site commemorates the noted Bursledon shipbuilder, George Parsons, who was responsible for building "The Elephant" in 1744, Nelson's flagship at the Battle of Copenhagen. When George Parsons failed to obtain renewal of his lease on this site, he moved his sheds, equipment, workmen and all to the site of the present boatyard at Warsash. He built his men cottages and an inn, the 'Sun', later replaced by the present 'Rising Sun'.

'The Jolly Sailor', now on our right hand side was originally a flat fronted house with sash windows – the present bow windows are a comparatively recent addition. Until it was sold and modernised, it was a little waterfront pub where on winter evenings perhaps a dozen 'locals' congregated and at closing time had to negotiate the steep path up to the road above roof level.

Bursledon waterside

1930's view of the river from Jolly Sailor

'Myrtle Cottage', next to 'The Jolly Sailor', was for some years the abode of Bill James, who looked like a W.W. Jacobs character, pipe and all. He always stood at the oars, and thus had a much better view of things as he propelled his dinghy along.

There was a ship's figurehead of a woman in the garden, looking over the river, and this was repainted from time to time, but always with a dead white face. A little rouge would have made such a difference to her! Mrs. James' father, Captain Willsher, a fine looking old seaman, was the previous occupant of the cottage.

Then there is the 'Elephant Boatyard', run by Mr. Michael Richardson and his sons. This is part of the site of the slipways where the wooden battleships were built, including "The Elephant". The name of the boatyard today, commemorates that ship and uses an elephant as its sign.

Philemon Ewer's house, 'Ewers', is just alone here on the waterfront and this family also owned 'Upcott' at one time. Philemon and his son, another Philemon, were shipbuilders and had their business at Bursledon and Cowes on the Isle of Wight. Another interesting owner of 'Ewers' was Mr. W. Scoresby Routledge, the explorer and anthropologist.

He and his wife sailed from Southampton in 1913 in the schooner "Mana" (91 tons) and, after five months, arrived at Easter Island to study the giant statues and other archeological objects there, remaining there until August, 1915, at which time they rather belatedly discovered that there was a war in progress. They arrived back in England in 1916, having covered 100,000 miles under sail, for which they were awarded the Royal Cruising Challenge Cup which had previously been held by Lord Brassey's "Sunbeam".

Station Hill, Bursledon. Boxwood Cottage (on Left) has been demolished

Leaving the 'Elephant Boatyard' we proceed down Station Hill which, before the railway came was known as North Hill, and now fortunately, DOWN only, thus preventing the alarming confrontations which used to take place on the bend at the top, when one or other vehicle had to back, either round the corner or down the length of the narrow hill.★ The main hazard now is ice in the winter, because water seeps from the field behind 'Upcott' and has nowhere to run except down the road.

★NOTE Hill now closed to traffic.

Thomas Ekless bought 'Upcott' from the Ewer family for £500 with all the land down to the river (there was no railway embankment then).

Upcott Bursledon

Bursledon Railway Station & riverside 1890

'Upcott' still has a wonderful view over Bursledon Pool although the car park and railway lines (no longer the station though) have been interposed between it and the river. The internal panelling was probably done by Thomas Ekless as he was a shipwright by trade. The grandson of Thomas, John Iremonger Ekless, lived in it from 1790 to 1869 and considered it 'one of the most delightful places in all England'.

John Ekless was a very public spirited man, who did a great deal of good; obtaining pardons from William IV and George IV for local men transported for their part in the Agricultural Riots; he was instrumental in getting a church built at Sarisbury Green and his labourers dug the foundations for it. He worked earnestly for thirty years to have many of its harshest features removed from the Poor Law Act. Another example of his generosity was when two or three hundred emigrants on their way to America were rescued from a sinking ship and landed at Southampton destitute, he 'undertook their cause, gathered together clothing and money, escorted them to Liverpool, and paid for berths on board a good seaworthy ship for such of them as were disposed to go on, and also paid expenses of those disheartened by their misfortunes, who decided to return whence they had come'.

His tombstone is just by the porch at St. Leonard's Church and the lengthy obituary notices in the Hampshire newspapers of the time bear witness to the number of people who remembered his every deed. The papers also reported that 'the late Lord Palmerston was wont to listen to Mr. Ekless's observations with regard to the agricultural labourers with a great deal of interest, his lordship knowing full well that he took a real interest in their welfare and that they were a class of man he had studied for a long period and for whose benefit he had so assiduously worked'.

John married, at Titchfield in 1812, the daughter of Captain William Preston, whose brother, Levi Preston, commanded the "Admiral Barrington"

Bursledon Pool 1909

(1782), the first ship to the relief of the beleaguered garrison at Gibraltar. Mrs. Ekless's mother lived at Sarisbury Green, where she gave much money to the church, and died at the age of ninety, in 1840.

Another sidelight was John's fondness for animals – he had a dog named Keeper, and on their walks a favourite cat would sometimes follow, and 'when scared by strangers would dart into the hedge and await our return'. If we take the footpath which he would have used from 'Upcott' on his way to church, we can look from the shadow of the woodland down the valley of the creek which was once there, by which the French monks came when travelling from Hamble to Bursledon. We can still climb the steps leading from their landing place to the church. The monks were allocated the land by Henry de Blois, Bishop of Winchester, who instructed them to build a chapelry at Brixedona, 'serve it well, and repair it'. They also built a church at Hound in the same simple style, with no transepts. St. Leonard's with its Early English arching, is believed to have been constructed about 1230, but there probably was an earlier building on this site. One of the reasons for such a theory is that the Norman font has carving extending around half its perimeter, as though it once stood half concealed in a corner. It has been completed with Early English carving which possibly was done when the font was moved to a more prominent position in the later church.

St. Leonards, Bursledon,
the old shipbuilders' church & font.

10

In 1341, Edward III took possession of Hamble Priory and its outlying chapels, and William of Wykham acquired Bursledon and Hound churches to provide revenue for his College of St. Mary at Winchester.

The transepts at St. Leonard's were built in the period 1885-96 to replace two 'mean' transepts with galleries which had been erected in 1833. The silver 'Challis' owned by the church was thought, until recently, to be Elizabethan, but is now known to have been included in an inventory during the reign of Edward VI.
One bell bears an inscription 'In God Is My Holp' and was cast in 1625 by John Higden, and the second bell was cast by Mears of Whitechapel in 1838 and

presented to the church by Commander T.W.Oliver R.N., who lived at 'Oak Hill' (now the 'Crows Nest').
The memorial tablets to Philemon Ewer and George Parsons, the shipbuilders, are interesting, and there are others to Philemon's grand-daughter, Celia, and to George Parson' descendants, the Rubies.

Half way down Station Hill stood the original Boxwood Cottage. The last owner before it was demolished was Mrs. Osborne, a dear little rosy-apple of a woman of ninety odd. She and her sister had been stewardesses on the liners out of Southampton in the hey-day of sea voyaging, and they had that air of comforting assurance that such a calling needed.

DEACONS BOATYARD

In years gone by there were slipways across what is now Station Road, but, if we could fly over the railway embankment here, we should find slipways now in Deacons Boatyard.
Francis Deacon had been brought up at Reading and spent all his spare time on the River Thames.
He went through the Great War, and, when it ended in 1918, he was a patient in the Royal Victoria Hospital at Netley, and there met his future wife.
After a few preliminary ventures, one of which was producing a weekly football paper, "The Hampshire Sporting Times", from an office in St. Michael's Street, Southampton, he bought a strip of foreshore below Bursledon Railway Station in 1922, cleared some of the bushes, and started his yard with one small shed and a 70ft. ex. M.L. "Mayfly" on which they lived for some years. Subsequently he bought 'Upcott' on Station Hill, originally owned by another shipbuilding family, as we have seen, and just previously used as the Stationmaster's house.
One of the regular jobs at the yard for the first few years was the spreading of chalk. The object was to

raise the level of the marshy land, fill in hollows and consolidate the ground. The old Southern Railway Company was very co-operative in this matter, as part of the yard was leased from them, and they sent train loads of chalk which were tipped down the embankment from the trucks, and easy way of delivery. According to Mr. Reg Moody , when the embankment was first made it all slid into the river one night... and certainly when a heavy train passed by the yard one could feel the ground shake.

Mr. & Mrs F.J. Deacon.
1932

Above
W.G. (Bill) Richards, who was Deacon's yard foreman for many years, and during Mrs Deacons' widowhood.

The yard prospered, mainly due to the friendly attitude of the workpeople and the owner towards the customers, who enjoyed the freedom of the yard after their city life. The office was on the upper deck of an old barge/houseboat, with large windows giving a splendid view of Bursledon Pool, and the difficulty was to get callers to go....

As the thirties proceeded, and the situation in Hitler's Germany looked ever more threatening, a yacht with a slow diesel thumped its way up the Hamble. On board were two dental surgeons, man and wife, the vessel laden with their most precious possessions, and all their dental equipment. They were eventually able to set up in practice, and in the winter of 1982/3 died in Southampton within a few weeks of one another, both aged over eighty - one refugee story which turned out well.

Strange people appear in boatyards, as elsewhere, and appearances are deceptive. The Yard did once, unwittingly, harbour a band of smugglers... An ex-officer type applied for a mooring for a fairly large motor vessel, and was allocated a berth afloat. He gave an address a little way up-country, and it was noticed vaguely that friends went out with him sometimes and they landed at the jetty with several suitcases, but no-one thought anything about it until one day when the whole affair broke in the newspapers. Afterwards it was one of the prosecutions quoted in a book written by a retired Collector of Customs, entitled "Anything to Declare".

By 1939 there were many yachts on the Hamble, and they had to be brought ashore and immobilised. The yards were then faced with the end of private work, and an interval before Admiralty contracts came through. Francis Deacon, determined to keep his men employed, even had the fitters making ploughshares, a national need, but one which was extremely unprofitable! However, it all sorted itself out in time, Deacons men were kept busy throughout the war with the overhaul of steam pinnaces from Portsmouth Dockyard. The team was in the charge of Lieut. F. Paton-Moore, a retired

officer who was an expert on this type of machinery (the same person who invented the Kestraphone, and will be mentioned later on). They also slipped and repaired Landing Craft, of which there were many in the river, the woods upstream concealing a Royal Marines Base, H.M.S. "Cricket".

War damage at Deacon's consisted of a large boatshed and contents destroyed by incendiary bombs one night, and a machine-gunning attack by a low flying daylight raider which sank one boat. Francis Deacon died in 1950, having seen his yachting business grown increasingly since the war, and having, with his boatyard neighbours, put the Regatta back on the calendar as an important local event. His widow carried on the yard for a further eleven years, with the old staff in the charge of her late husband's foreman, Mr. W.G. (Bill) Richards. Eventually the yard was sold as there was no family to continue.

The interior of the original office at Deacons Boatyard, on the upper deck of a barge. F.J. Deacon is on the extreme left.

When Mrs. Deacon was left the yard she was not the first or last woman to be in this situation. In 1693 Anne Wyatt became a widow, and conducted a spirited campaign to recover from the Naval authorities the money owed to her late husband for the building of H.M.S. "Devonshire". It would be nice to know a great deal more about Anne Wyatt. Her husband, William, died of smallpox when he was only thirty-nine, so she was presumably under

the age of fifty when she conducted her battle with the Admiralty paymasters, and to obtain contracts for the construction of other vessels. Did she journey to London for this purpose? If so, it was quite an undertaking – a ferry across the river, then by rough track to Fareham or Portsmouth, and onward by coach to London. The foreman, Richard Herring, would deal with the yard in her absence, and perhaps one of the kinsmen would go with her.

How interesting if she had kept a diary, as did Celia Fiennes who was related to the Wyatts and visited them at Bursledon, as also did Daniel Defoe. The Wyatt's daughter married Sir Jasper Culham of Hawstead, Suffolk, so they must all have travelled the country in spite of the difficulties.

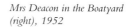

Mrs Deacon in the Boatyard (right), 1952

The next owner of Deacon's Yard was a woman too. Mrs. Sheridan was a mother of children who sailed Optimist dinghies at Bursledon (which was when the idea of buying a boatyard occurred to her), and the owner of a pack of Cavalier King Charles spaniels. These enjoyed life by the river, and on cold wet days, elegantly occupied the best places in the various offices, close by the heaters. Mrs. Sheridan, affectionately known as 'Hurricane Lavinia', was full of ideas, The roadway was raised above normal tide-levels, new sheds were built over the sedge, and the old barge/office was demolished. In the next few years yachts were built to the designs of Fred Parker of Warsash, Chris Holman and James McGruer.

The yard was resold in 1966 to the Granary Group, who leased the chandlery to J.G. Meakes Ltd. and later brought other companies to the site.

Mention must be made here of the little yard of Primmer & Snook, which was established beside Bursledon Bridge (in what is now part of Deacon's Yard) in about 1920, and continued for forty years or so, until Ern Primmer died and Mr. Snook retired. They built very good dinghies and small craft of the traditional wooden construction. They had a real Heath Robinson steaming arrangement for bending timber, in the open, alongside the fence which in those days separated their yard from Deacon's driveway, so that it was in full view of interested spectators.

Their office was a wooden shed so crammed with shelves full of papers that there was no room for any customer to enter, he would be obliged to stand on the step and conduct his business from there, and on high spring tides the whole area would be flooded and the workmen would have to sit on the top of their benches.

They were a very honest pair, and when Francis Deacon started up his yard he assured them that there need be no rivalry. From then on the two businesses worked side by side, and each consulted the other on any matters which affected the general good and they never attempted to lure away the others customers. It was a gentleman's agreement, honourably kept.

Beyond, across the river, is Moody's Yard and the huge Swanwick Marina. This boatyard has been owned by the same family for a hundred and fifty years, the sixth generation now being in the business. It was started in about 1827 by John Moody a carpenter who started boatbuilding in the back yard of his cottage at Swanwick and them moved to a small parcel of land on Swanwick Shore. He was joined by his son, Alexander, in about 1850. They repaired fishing boats and built dinghies and small craft. There were very few yachts about in those days.

Alexander Herbert Moody (known always as Herbert), and his brother Frederick, worked with their father until his retirement.

A partnership known as A.H. & F. Moody was then created, and remained so until 1930 when Frederick retired. The brothers had a writer named Mr Ernest Beale who sent out the accounts in beautiful copperplate handwriting. Each partner always consulted the other before giving any decision to an enquiring customer – it was all done in a very proper and business-like manner. Mr Harold Daish was the foreman engineer.

Reginald Moody joined this partnership in about 1907. For many years but mainly during the time of Mr. Reg Moody, Mr. Bundy of Bursledon was Yard Foreman. He was much esteemed by countless yachtsmen who mentioned him in the books of their cruises, and expressed their gratitude for his advice and help in the preparation for their departures. From the start of the company there has been a progression of property purchases, and now the site extends to approximately 17 acres.

Early days at Moodys on Swanwick shore.
Mr A. H. Moody (with coil of rope)

Below: Swanwick Shore before the Marina

The 1960s saw the beginning of the Moody Swanwick Marina development which is now complete, having been carried out in stages. The building of wooden yachts was discontinued and now the company completes glass fibre hulls as well as carrying out repairs and refits, and having successful New Boat Sales, Brokerage and Chandlery departments.

During the 1914/18 war Reg was called to work at Camper & Nicholson's Yard, so Herbert and Frederick carried on, with two or three elderly employees – the main task at this time being to remove lead keels and ballast for the war effort. Another job which Moody's Yard carried out regularly in those days was the repair and maintenance of the old wooden Bursledon Bridge. This ceased to be their responsibility in the early 1930s when it was demolished and replaced by the new concrete bridge. Alan R. Moody began his apprenticeship as an engineer with the firm in 1928 and continued in the Fitting Shop for two years, after which he moved to the office, becoming Chairman and Director of the new company: A.H.Moody & Son, in August 1935.

In 1935, the firm was almost wholly engaged in yacht repairs, but then followed the building of the first yacht, "Vindilis", for Dr. Harrison Butler, a well known amateur designer. This was followed, until the outbreak of war, by a considerable number of well known yachts.
In turn A. H. Moody's Grandsons, Roy Williamson, Eric and Gordon Moody followed Alan into the family firm.

During the Second World War some 120 craft of all types, including sixteen 72ft. M.L.s were built, and repairs and modifications carried out to more than 2,000 Admiralty vessels.

Among the Ministry craft to begin their careers on the Hamble was the X3, the first midget submarine – which was later to be involved in the sinking of the "Tirpitz". X3 was launched on Sunday 15th March 1943, having been 'on the stocks' for the best part of three years, and she went through her many trials here on the Hamble until late August of that year when she was transferred to Faslane in Scotland. She was built (and to a large part designed) by Commander Varley at his company : Varley Marine Ltd. John Lorimer, one of the first crew members of the new project, and at that time a newly commissioned Midshipman RNVR, wrote at that period:

I remember the great day when David Locket and I went down to the yard on the Hamble to see the first, the only X-craft, HMS/MX3. We were shown over by Don Cameron, and I remember thinking how incredibly small everything looked and wondering how such a frail craft was expected to cross the North Sea.

The next day I went on my first trip . It was just a surface run… During the next three weeks we went over to the Hamble occasionally, but X3 spent most of her time in the big shed where she was built, while various Admiralty experts arrived, trying to sell their various instruments, most of which could not even be got inside the craft.

Commander Varley (who incidentally had retired from the Royal Navy before the Second World War but was always known as 'Commander' thereafter), and Commander Bell were later jointly commemorated in the naming of the first midget submarine shorebase, H.M.S. Varbel in Scotland.

The 'Swan' (now Mulligan's) was on the corner of Church Lane and Bridge Road. The first 'Swan' on this site stood on what is now the car park, and faced the river. The pub was always a very busy meeting place and was certainly so in the 1939/45 war, the landlord, Roderick Skiff, being a very popular man who commanded the local Home Guard. The Home Guard took part in night exercises with a troop of Commandos who were billeted locally.

Frank Verrill, who had an engineering business in Deacon's Yard, was the man who once took a swan to the 'Swan'! A half grown cygnet appeared at the yard, driven off by its parents. Frank fed it every day and made it a shelter under a boat. It followed him about, and so one day he tucked it under his arm and took it across to the bar, where it was given bread and water, and was photographed by a passing 'Echo' man, appearing in that night's edition of the paper...It left the yard eventually but returned some months later with its mate, and waddled ashore to see Frank... evidently a very satisfied customer!

Bridge Road, Bursledon and the old Swan Inn

There used to be six cottages near the 'Swan' in Church Lane. These had looked directly onto the river in the days before the railway embankment was made, and high tides lapped their doorsteps. Their footings were of the granite which had come from Cornwall and the Channel Islands as ballast in the sailing coasters, and which is also to be seen at 'Dolphin House' (15th Century), the 'Old Cottage' in High Street, and in the stable yard of 'The White House'. The six cottages are all gone now and the site is occupied by a block of flats.

Retracing our footsteps along Station Road and then up Station Hill we'll make for the High Street. We pass the brick wall on our right which guards 'Greyladyes Park' and here is the gateway of 'Greywell'. The entrance to this house is now through this gateway at the side, although, when it was a public house known as the 'New Inn'. it fronted onto the road.

The New Inn (now Greywell), Bursledon

Cottages (now demolished) in Church Lane. Note the stone footings brought as ballast in milling coasters.

Here, at the fork where High Street and Lands End Road meet, is 'Yew Trees', a very ancient house in which, for generations, whoever held the post of Head Gardener of the 'Greyladyes' estate (earlier known as 'Elm Lodge') always lived.

John Hallett (the last of the estate gardeners) and his wife, Laura, celebrated their diamond wedding at 'Yew Trees' when they were 84 and 85 respectively. Mrs. Hallett had been born at 'Yew Trees' as her father had been Farm Bailiff in 1878 when the estate was owned by the Humphreys family.

Across the road at 'Dale Cottage' lived Captain Alfred James, who went to sea at fourteen and could remember well the days when six or seven square rigged vessels at a time lay in the river loading cargo.

At the green in High Street we turn right and follow the wall of 'Greyladyes' round. Back in 1800 this estate was called 'Bursledon Lodge' and was the home of the Trench family. There is a memorial tablet to the father, Richard Trench, in the north transept of St. Leonard's Church, erected by his three sons. He was born in Ireland in 1774, is recorded as one of the investors in the Itchen Bridge Company

Mr John Hallet, head gardener at Greyladyes about 1930

in 1834, and died at Botley Hill in 1860. His wife, Melisina, died in 1827 and there is a memorial to her in Winchester Cathedral. Her son, Francis, wrote

We remember her efforts on behalf of the suffering slaves, the suffering chimney boys, the suffering Irish, boys and children suffering any cruel treatment, boys killed in school fights (?) and others without end, among rich and poor, in any part of the world.

Evidently a very sensitive and compassionate lady.

August 26th 1831, Upton Cottage, Bursledon. I remained some days at Chessel, and now at this delightful spot which I always like. I have seen our old tutor, Pritchard, old King and his wife, and several of the Bursledon villagers. They all asked after you affectionately.

This letter was written by Francis Trench to his father, after his mother's death and when Richard Trench had left Bursledon. The mention of 'our old tutor, Pritchard', may link him with the Dame Pritchard under whose care John Ekless had his first

Old Bursledon has much elaborate brickwork - walls and chimneys. The house in the background is Greywell, originally the New Inn

Lower end of High Street, Old Bursledon. 1907 Centre - 'Yew Trees'

lessons. Another son, Richard Chenevix Trench, born 1807, died 1886, was in turn, curate of Alverstoke, vicar of Itchen Stoke, vicar of Curdridge, and finally, Archbishop of Dublin. He wrote" The Study of Words" and other books and hymns.

Francis Trench published a book, "Notes from the Past", when he was Rector of Islip, Oxfordshire in 1862, and the references to Bursledon quoted are from his letters to his parents:

Greyladyes. 1906

What a contrast Oxfordshire and the beautiful coast of Hampshire, and especially our own neighbourhood with its woods, coppices, commons, and interesting waters all combined in such exquisite variety and loveliness. Here, we have white, pasty, muddy soil in exchange for the dry rich coloured gravel of our roads, drives, and walks about dear old Bursledon.

The two Angelus Bells at Greyladyes R.C. Chapel

Cottages now 'Ladymead'

Later in the 19th Century the house was owned by the Humphreys family and was known as 'Elm Lodge'. Then it passed into the ownership of Mrs. Emmaline Shawe-Storey who gave its present name.

She was passionately fond of beautiful brickwork and when she bought several of the local houses she rebuilt a number of the chimneys on them. She bought properties around the perimeter of her estate, modernised them and then let them. These include in their number: the 'New Inn', now 'Greywell', Hackett's Farmhouse, which is now 'Lattice Cottage' in High Street, 'The Grange', 'Barn Court', and other houses in that complex which were farm buildings. There used to be a pond in the middle of the courtyard and Mrs. Hallett of 'Yew Trees' remembered when one of the children who lived in the farmhouse was drowned in it.

Mrs. Shawe-Storey became a Roman Catholic and in 1906 provided and furnished the church of Our Lady of the Rosary, to which came people from a wide area. (The late Mr.W.W.Fox said that it was originally the ballroom of the big house). Mrs. Shawe-Storey died in 1937 and the house was occupied by troops during the war, but the chapel continued, although damp caused much deterioration. The splendid organ was removed to St. Patrick's at Woolston, and after the war, when the house was sold, the Woolston Catholic Community bought the chapel, so that it has continued its services. When the roof was renewed in 1980/81 the congregation was invited to use St. Leonard's Parish Church, which they did for some time.

Originally there were two Angelus bells hanging where now can be seen only the one, which were rung at 7am, twelve noon and 6pm by one of the estate workers, but during the war a Royal Marines reveller unhooked one bell from its anchorage so that it was broken.

*Looking down the High Street.
Cottages on right are now gone.*

*Old Bursledon
High Street,
looking towards
the Vine.
Old Cottage is on
the right*

The tiny overgrown burial plot with the vandalised mausoleum, on the bend in Church Lane, was also part of the estate; Captain Shawe-Storey being buried there.

The estate had its own brewery on land between the 'Bell House' and 'Ladymead' (the latter of these two being enlarged and improved almost out of all recognition by the Mrs. Shawe-Storey). The row opposite 'Ladymead' included a part named St. Benet's Hall, to which the writer can remember being invited to see a pantomime one Christmas a very long time ago.

At the junction of School Road and High Street, there is an old shop, now sadly no longer in business. In days gone by housekeeping was a very different affair to today. There were no supermarkets or hypermarkets around and no general means of getting about or transporting heavy loads of shopping, beyond a horse and trap, or the train if you happened to live within reach of the railway.

Therefore the country shops 'waited upon families', as their billboards put it - which meant that a man called for orders, and the goods were later delivered to your door. Groceries, meat, bread, all appeared. A Southampton chemist even sent an elderly man wearing a bowler hat, riding a pedalled contraption with a heavy box on the front, containing an assortment of patent medicines and toiletry; the whole thing rather on the lines of the later ice-cream 'stop-me-and-buy-one' machines. The milk came in churns aboard a very smart pony trap, and was dipped out in shining metal measures into the customers' jug by the pretty daughters of the dairyman. The Old Bursledon shop cum Post Office did a very good trade in those days, and kept busy the proprietors, Mr. and Mrs. Rayment, two of their three sons, an assistant in the Post Office section, and sometimes another person too. The Rayments also owned the row of four cottages (now demolished) up the street from the shop, and the strawberry field where the house 'Hamull' now stands.

Mrs. Rayment was the driving force behind the business and the main competition was from the old established firms of Lankester and Crook of Woolston and branches, and of Maffey in Botley Square. They sent their bowler-hatted travellers around the district once a week, and delivered the goods later. Maffey supplied drapery and haberdashery as well, but the Rayments also had a shop at Lowford which stocked ribbons and useful household goods so honours were even. Mr. Rayment drove a horse and trap and acted as liaison between the two. He also attended auction sales. He was a nice man but, unfortunately, suffered from rheumatism in his legs so that he rolled from side to side as he walked. Their son, Hubert, was the survivor of all the people who lived in the High Street row - he only left in 1982 when he was old and the last cottage was then demolished.

Other tenants had included John Harding who was for years verger at the church, and his grandson, John Armstrong, who was organist at one period. In another of the cottages had lived the mother of Mary Wheeler who was Mrs. Shawe-Storey's head housemaid at 'Greyladyes'. The shop was eventually closed in 1981 and made into a residence but the shop frontage is still retained.

The 'Old Cottage', opposite the shop, was originally thatched, and then was occupied by members of the Fox family. Foxes and Fishers were very numerous among the local strawberry growing community and connected by marriage with a goodly proportion of the other inhabitants.

'The Dolphin', which stands on the corner of Salterns Lane, used to be an alehouse. It still has the ornamental bracket above its lovely square 15th Century porch where the sign used to hang. After 'The Dolphin' gave up its licence to 'The Vine', a Scottish family named Robertson lived in the house for some time and carried on a coal merchants business there. The yard was larger than it is now, because the original house was square, on either side of the old porch. It had the wing to the Salterns side of the house added in 1930.

At 'The White House', which used to be called 'The Lawn', lived the late Mr. C.F. Fox of the Hampshire Field Society. In 1888, when the foundations for the new vestry at St. Leonard's church were dug, what was obviously a common grave was discovered, containing the skeletons of large men who had apparently died in battle. Mr. Fox, after many discussions with Barney Sutton, who helped dig the foundations and remembered the skeletons vividly, was convinced they were Vikings defeated by Alfred in AD897, and not victims of the Plague.

The Dolphin with innkeepers
Mr and Mrs Winter (probably about 1878)

*Mr and Mrs James Spencer
of Walnut Cottage,
Old Bursledon, on the
occasion of their
Diamond Wedding
in the 1930's*

Walnut Cottage at the top end of High Street

'Walnut Cottage' (on the corner of Salterns Lane) was once divided into three and each portion was let to a married couple in their 80s. When a survey was carried out in the thirties it was found that, including these six people, there were twenty-seven inhabitants of Old Bursledon, all active, and whose combined average age was 78. Indeed, villagers Mr. and Mrs. James Spencer celebrated their diamond wedding at 'Walnut Cottage'.

Turning down Salterns Lane, we come to the other and much later 'Bursledon Lodge'. This house was built in 1920 by Sir Mansfield Smith Cumming, head of the Boom Defence, and was later owned by Mr. Noel van Raalte, who was a first class engineer. He was carefully chosen by W.O.Bentley to try out the new 3-litre Bentley car in 1921, Mr. Bentley wrote in his autobiography that if there were any weak spots in the car they were confident that these would show up in the hands of van Raalte. During his ownership of 'Bursledon Lodge' the boatyard on the marsh was used for the building of small experimental skimming boats, like sea sledges, each powered by an outboard motor. These raced off Hythe on Saturdays and attained very high speeds. Sir Charles Segrave, the racing motorist, and Mr. Hubert Scott-Paine of the Power Boat Company were among those who 'had a go'. Mr. van Raalte also had a high speed cruiser, "Mariette", which provided him with a study in the use of duralumin

and new metals in salt water, and later his "Flying Fish" was a familiar sight on the river. He died in 1940, and 'Bursledon Lodge' was taken over by Folland Aircraft to disperse some of their office work from the factory at Hamble, in view of the nightly bombings at that time. When the war ended the house was divided and others built in the grounds, as was the fate of all the large buildings in the area. As a little aside: Mr. van Raalte's father, Mr. Charles van Raalte, owned Brownsea Island in Poole Harbour, where the first Boy Scouts camp was held in 1907.

Salterns Lane leads down to the marshes and the previously mentioned Badnam Creek. In about 1906 several old Naval ships: "Argo", "Melita", "Mutine", "Asov" and others, arrived in the river off Badnam with the Admiralty Boom Defence men who had been engaged for some time in experiments in Southampton Water. These consisted of blocking off the port with booms, against which a destroyer was run to test the strength and effectiveness of the blockage which could be used in wartime conditions.

To make access for the crews of these ships a pier was built across the marshes from the bottom of Salterns Lane, and the seaward end was finished off with a platform around the mast of the old battleship "Sultan". The mast was brought from Portsmouth Dockyard aboard a ship, and tilted to heel into the mud. Such is the softness of the Hamble mud that its own weight took the mast down until half its length was submerged, and the sailors found fresh water in the depths inside it. The mast remained as a feature of the river for years, only being taken down when the pier was immobilised (sections removed) at the beginning of the Second World War. The Harbour Board subsequently put the present marker on the site.

Many of the men on these ships were from Portsmouth and when returning from leave had quite a walk up hill from Bursledon Railway Station, calling in at 'The Vine' in High Street before continuing on down Salterns Lane to the pier. The inhabitants of Old Bursledon viewed the arrival of what they feared would be a lot of rough sailors in the early 1900s with some concern – fortunately the reality was not so bad!

Until the 1920s there were only a few houses in Salterns Lane. After passing by the pond there was a pair named Lince Grove at the bend of the lane, the cottage now enlarged as Clouds Hill, and between these was a tiny single storied cottage where Hiram Willsher, one of the old villagers, his daughter and her husband, four little girls and a boy, lived. Really a close family...

The path to the marsh, from Salterns Lane

On down the lane was the house, 'Salterns', where George Parsons, the shipbuilder, lived from 1793 until his death there in 1812. Beside it stood the old barn and the giant oak tree. Opposite was the lime avenue leading to 'Brownhill'.

The mast of the 'Sultan' on the occasion of its positioning to form the end of the Boom Defence Pier. 'Bridgewater House' in the background 1906

George Parsons was born at Poole in 1729 and was apprenticed to a Portsmouth shipbuilder in the year 1744. The first record of him having a yard of his own is in the Navy Board letter of December 9th 1778 to the Lords Commissioners of the Admiralty, notifying an offer from Mr. George Parsons to build, in his yard at Bursledon, a ship of 32 guns. This offer was accepted – a 'Man o'War' of 689 tons at £11.10.0 per ton, to be launched early in 1780 – being the terms of the contract.

Thinking of the barn at Salterns reminds me that when Captain Cumming was called to London at the outbreak of the 1914 War a good deal of the furniture from Bridgewater House was put into the barn for storage. I was allowed to borrow books and, apart from "Children of the New Forest", I read the whole set of Captain Marryat's seafaring novels, (bound in red leather and somewhat nibbled by mice), by the time I was ten years old. Fortunately in those days publishers were much more careful of what they printed, and the swear words used by the characters were represented by long dashes in the text! He also wrote one book, "Monsieur Violet", about the American Indians, which you never see nowadays.

It was interesting, years later, when I visited Chewton Glen, after it became an internationally known good food restaurant and hotel, to see the relics of Capt. Marryat in the house which had formerly belonged to his brother, and where he often stayed (1792/1848). It would have astonished him to see a helicopter land on the lawn, bringing a party to lunch, a whirling insect-like contraption. R.A.Calvert said that Senhor Cierva always became annoyed when his auto-giro was cast in the part of a clown at air pageants; his invention saved countless lives from shipwrecks and other disasters, and has certainly proved its usefulness.

In the other direction from 'Walnut Cottage' is Kew Lane - the name probably deriving from the Saxon-Germanic word *skew* meaning crooked. The first house in Kew Lane was occupied Miss Edith Otway, a schoolmistress of the local Infants School, a tiny woman with her hair drawn back in a knot, who was regarded with affection and respect by all the village. The parents never questioned her authority over the children in her care, in fact most of them had been her 'infants' in their turn. She had an old, bedridden mother, and an elderly brother, George Otway, who did woodworking jobs on the 'Greyladyes' estate. So, with these two and the children, she was never idle. Her sole personal pleasure – which one imagines must have been taken out of sheer self-preservation – was to catch the train to Southampton on Saturday afternoons and go to the pictures - the first silent films - Charlie Chaplin, Mary Pickford, Fatty Arbuckle, Lilian Gish and the other stars of that period. When Miss Otway retired she went to live in Surrey, and as she lasted until well over her ninetieth birthday, it is safe to assume that she saw many of the later 'talkies'. After she left Bursledon, the cottage was in succession, modernised, thatched, burnt out, rebuilt, and is now tiled, so that it does not at all resemble the original. A footpath to Netley and Hamble runs alongside, and in this field by the hedge, was a shed in which Barney Sutton, he who dug the foundations of the new vestry and found Vikings' skeletons, spent his leisure hours - sitting in the wheelbarrow which served as his armchair!

One of the Naval personnel who came to Bursledon with the Boom Defence in 1906 was my father, Robert Ritchie. He and my mother rented 'Orchard House' in Kew Lane (since demolished and 'Wayside' now occupies part of the site). Before my father arrived, the tenant had been the village schoolmaster and organist, Samuel Wright. He was a very energetic, quick-tempered, musical man and on Sundays could be seen during the sermon, lurking behind a pillar, shaking his fist at some choirboy who was misbehaving - and no doubt retribution would come on

H.M.S. "ARGO" a Boom Defence ship

Monday morning when the delinquent was back in class. Mrs. Wright played the organ for the Childrens' Service on Sunday afternoons, and took piano pupils at the house to which they moved, opposite the old school. With such a couple in control the church music was in very good hands, and the Rector could safely leave it to them. They also rehearsed and staged an operetta each winter in the village hall.

The Fox and Hounds with Pilands Wood in the background, before the Barn was set up behind the pub

The trees at 'Orchard House' had obviously been planted around 1860 or thereabouts, since they were very large and in no way resembled the pruned rods and bushes which grow in present day gardens. There were black 'Merry' cherries, which, when cooked, were quite delicious, 'Whiteheart' cherries, old varieties of apple, including the red 'Quarendens' and the red and green 'Deux Ans', which kept until March and in spite of the suggestion of only a bi-annual crop, always bore large quantities of fruit, and several trees of 'William' pears. There is just one day when a 'William' pear is at its peak of perfection, so they were spread out on an upper landing and every evening we would pick out those which were 'just right'.

My father persuaded the village lads to come and ask for fruit rather than continuing their practice of hurling stones at the trees near the lane and the footpath, and this they did. One boy, John Sutton, came for years for 'peers' as he called them.

The grass was allowed to grow undisturbed until June, when a man named Brock scythed it (a very skilful performance) and carted it to Hungerford for his animals. The fruit blossom in the spring made the garden a fairyland and in the winter the gales brought down old limbs which burnt fragrantly in the open fireplaces. The orchard marked the seasons, and is a very pleasant memory.

Kew Lane, which bears round to the right from the top of old Bursledon High Street and presently skirts the side of a little hill with Hungerford Valley below it, is said to be an ancient British trackway. It is a very pretty narrow lane and has undoubtedly looked much the same for centuries. In the period from about 1900 to 1930 there were only four houses in it. 'Bondfield', and the other three houses and land between, belonged to a retired doctor, Henry Parsons (there seems to be no connection with the shipbuilding family of the same name). He was a perfectionist and freely expressed the view that if you want something done properly you must do it yourself.... His niece, a sweet, dithery, little lady, kept house for him, with the aid of cook and parlourmaid. The latter must have been one of the first road casualties due to the motor car – she was killed whilst riding her bicycle to a neighbouring village to visit her family. The doctor – in the mid nineteen twenties – bought a nice new motor car and then complained that there was nowhere to go! This, with all England spread out before him and comparatively empty of any traffic at that period. His niece used to tell a terrible tale of how they had arrived at a crossroads just a few minutes before another vehicle, it was quite shattering, what a narrow escape they had had! Not surprisingly the car soon disappeared from their coach–house.

The little valley of Hungerford, on a tributary stream of the Hamble, and where much of the ironwork for the old wooden battleships was made, was approachable by water in the days before the railway embankment was built across its outlet in 1888, and barges were able to gain access. With the end of Naval shipbuilding the ironworkers lost their occupation, and Hungerford in the early nineteen hundreds was a depressed area with some poor families in very substandard houses – one in fact was

right down by the stream where the footpath crosses on the way to Hamble. With the woods shading it and the water running by, it must have been terribly damp. The gamekeeper lived there.

All these old houses have long ago disappeared and there are now a number of new and attractive ones right up through the valley.

The 'Fox and Hounds' is the pub on the bottom road of the valley. It was there that 'Lovely Emma' was sold by her husband for a gallon of ale (shades of Thomas Hardy. Dorset was not the only place where this happened). The writer can remember having an old lady pointed out to her as 'Lovely Emma', so probably the event took place in the late eighteen hundreds. She remained with the man who bought her, and with all the divorce which goes on nowadays perhaps it is a little less shocking than it was then...

The slope behind the 'Fox and Hounds', where the modern houses are today, is called Pilands Wood, supposed to be named after the great number of magpies always seen there. The 16th Century barn, removed from a site near Winchester and patiently taken to pieces and reassembled by the Fanner Brothers for Don Taylor, who was then the proprietor of the 'Fox and Hounds', brings in many visitors to see the fine collection of old farm implements and country craft tools which are displayed and to have a little supper and a glass of

Strawberry Pickers

beer, particularly on a fine summer evening. Mr. W.G.Richards, told me that his grandfather worked for the Chamberlayne estate which owned the woods which stretched from behind Hungerford to Hamble, and he felled and prepared the timbers which were used in the building of the Fox and Hounds, and also in the Shamblehurst Barn which we pass on the way north to Winchester; one of the timbers there having his initials carved on it.

On the little hill at the head of Hungerford Valley is the 'Old Rectory' which was built in 1851 and was used for just over a hundred years. When an old bachelor, Mr. Lewin, lived there and protested that it was far too large and expensive to keep up, it was forsaken for the new Vicarage which was then built.

Amongst those who lived in turn in the 'Old Rectory' (and after whom roads are named in the new housing estate) was Canon Estridge, who took great interest in the children of the parish. During his time the church restoration took place, and he directed the carving of the font top and pulpit by local lads. The Canon was later appointed to Truro Cathedral, but, when he died, his body was brought back to Bursledon, where his gravestone may be seen at the far end of the old burial ground. Mr. Shirley was Rector before and during the First World War. He was a tall man with a dark beard, who wore a black straw 'boater', and called on all the parishioners regularly, (the population was very small compared to now). He had a large old English Sheepdog which lay outside any house where he was visiting, and at the church door when he was taking services. In the nineteen twenties there was Mr. Aubrey Cummins, to whom the people erected a commemorative plaque in the church. He was a sporting, outdoor type of parson, with a rugged countenance, and kept livestock – often he would be seen carrying a goose or a couple of ducks under his arm. He had come from Burley in the New Forest, and when he died suddenly he was taken back there for burial. There was great sadness in the village, and one poor wanderer named Charlie, whom the Rector had befriended, tramped the twenty or more miles to the funeral, deeply lamenting.

If we turn back towards the river, there is 'Ploverfield' where, until 1846, one of George Parsons' grandsons (another George) lived. At one time during its recent history it was a home for delinquent girls, then turned into three residences and those and the houses in its grounds were sold in the 1950s. Mrs. Gwen May remembers the time when she and her family lived at 'Mayfield' in the grounds of 'Ploverfield' in the mid fifties, her husband being in the RAF and stationed nearby. She vividly remembers how the travelling cinema used to arrive at Bursledon regularly on Wednesday evenings and set up for the full show in the village hall and then, at the end of the programme, pack everything away and disappear into the night again. She and her husband were among the founder members of the village drama group and used to rehearse and stage plays in the village hall. She recalls the many times when the Stage Manager and his team would be waiting in the 'wings' on a Wednesday evening to work into the night building the set for the next evening's dress rehearsal. The show must to on, they say!

A tradition of staged drama in the village, though, had been started years before – in the period 1918 onwards, when a family of players visited the village from time to time. They performed dramas such as "East Lynn" during the week, and on Saturdays "The Sleeping Beauty" or "Cinderella" for the children. Everybody took part, including the baby in arms. The village was also extremely proud of its Tug of War team, which travelled great distances and had an extremely fine record of success.

We can still leave Bursledon by train if we wish but nowadays we have to purchase tickets from a machine as the station buildings at Bursledon were taken down some time ago. In the years of the local strawberry industry (1879-1939) the station played a major part in this prosperity as the pony and donkey carts queued to off-load strawberry punnets into trains consisting of wagons with specially fitted shelving for the purpose. At the height of this era the 639 strawberry growers were producing 2270 tons of the fruit per year.

Brickmaking was a local industry, and it will be noticed that many of the houses have patterns of grey and red 'headers'. The Bursledon Brick Company factory is at Swanwick - two of the five chimneys are still there - one on each side of the motorway now - (the chimneys were locally known as 'the five sisters' by the brickmakers). Some of the old bricks probably came from little works up in the woods, of which traces could still be found up to a few years ago. However, the 'plenty of timber' to which Daniel Defoe once alluded, did not last for ever, because it came to light recently that there are many Bursledon bricks at Oakville in Ontario, apparently exported there in exchange for timber when the local stocks were badly depleted by the great demands of the shipbuilding community. Mr. Peter Page of Upton Lodge has a very interesting theory, borne out by an old map in his possession, that the northern boundary of Bursledon once extended across the river to include Burridge. This may account for the rather strange fact of the Bursledon Brickworks being on the 'wrong' side of the river now. Mr. Page also tells us that the Queen Elizabeth Country Park is properly in Hedge End, and that the old boundary stone in the wood was buried when the Royal Marines made their road from the camp to the water. This would be a little job for someone with an enquiring mind...

Between the motorway and the A27 on Providence Hill is the Bursledon windmill. Happily it is now in the care of the Hampshire Buildings Preservation Trust Limited and, in 1985 was restored as a working mill –about a hundred years since it last ground grain. The reason for its falling into disuse at that time –

just when it would in the normal course of events most probably have had its machinery changed to cast iron, as other mills did – is a domestic tale! The miller, Mr. Gosling, was forced to leap clear of the sails when they started to turn while he was working on them one day. As he was getting on in years, his wife, fearing for his life if other such mishaps occurred, persuaded him to retire. Although the mill stayed in the family until at least 1939, the mill was never worked again.

The first mill, a post mill, is thought to have been built hereabouts in 1740 and certainly appears on Admiralty charts as a navigational aid from at least 1782. The present structure, was built in 1813 and the first owner and miller was a woman, Phoebe Langtry.

The 18th century machinery, still well preserved, was luckily kept covered for, although the sails and cap had gone long ago, a platform was put across the top of the mill so that it could be used year after year as a vantage point from which the owners and their friends who were also interested in yacht racing could view the Solent events in the season. 'Upton Lodge', which is at the top of Blundells Lane, (the old road to Winchester,) is a lovely house incorporating part of an older manor. In fact Mr. C.F.Fox,linked it possibly with the manor of Robert de St. John, who died in 1266, as 'Hupton' held by the military tenure of one knight's fee. In more recent times it was 'Upton Farm' with land which extended over what is now the M37 Motorway to Oak Hill on the A27.

*A fancy dress party
from the VINE INN. 1919*

There are so many stories to be told about the river and the villages on it and the folk who lived and still live on and around the river.

During the nineteen twenties there were still some houseboats afloat in Bursledon Pool, the largest being the "Mary" of Salcombe owned by Sir Frederick Young. "Ferry House", the converted floating bridge, "Brilliant", the reputedly unlucky ship which Francis Deacon refused to buy when it was put on the market, even though he badly needed the mooring which went with it then, "Our Flat", a little square houseboat which appears in many of the early photographs, "Vanburgh" and "Eden", which Mr. Deacon did buy, and brought in onto the marsh as the Yard's first and most attractive office. The whole of the top deck accommodation had Vita glass round it, and was a splendid viewpoint, so that customers came, and stayed and stayed...

One of the last of the ex-Admiralty vessels to lie afloat here was M.L. 300, owned by Mr. Edmund Blakesley who lived on it all the year round. In winter he often had to fend off ice-floes which came down through the bridge on the ebb tide.

Leland, the 16th Century writer, said Hamble was a 'good fisshar town, with a haven, where yn is a very fair rode for great shippes'. Well, the great ships have sailed their way into history and planes have come and, as far as the Hamble is concerned today, gone, but the river still engages the joy and imagination of the World's sailors. As well as the people who sailed from the Hamble, years ago, and those who worked in the boatyards and allied trades beside it, the river attracted various odd characters who derived some solace from it. These folk had, like any community, some eccentrics. One man would drift about in a dinghy on nights of full moon, singing while his

dog companion howled in sympathy. Another made stew of the tiny crabs which abounded in the mud – and seemed to thrive on it. There was an elderly lady who lived on a boat with a large high powered engine, and when she felt the urge, would take off for the Isle of Wight, all by herself. The locals were so concerned that they would telephone the Harbour Master at whichever port she was headed for, and beg that someone would catch her mooring lines as she came in... Eventually she was persuaded by her anxious family to give up the sea and have a caravan... and everyone sighed with relief. The river people were a very caring community when there were fewer boats and more personal relationships.

It always surprises people who are not boatminded that sailing men will travel so far to enjoy a few hours on the water. Many people with craft on the Hamble River travel great distances to get there. Francis Deacon had an old friend who did this, and an auxiliary ketch was built for him at the yard, He was a quiet, gentle man whose wife refused to set foot on a boat, so she would sit in the car, while he went sailing. This, of course, restricted his cruising range. However, he managed, and then came 1939 and the war. By the time it was over he had become a widower and he was then free to go... However, he never went much further than the Isle of Wight, in company with two other old men with similar tastes. but it was wonderful to see his pleasure in these expeditions. The men at Deacon's Yard always tried to make things easy for him, because they liked him. However, two of the junior members were amused to find him one evening, pacing the jetty and pulling out his watch to gaze anxiously at it (rather like the white rabbit in "Alice in Wonderland").

Apparently he had lent his boat to someone for the day,

The wooded up-river reaches of the Hamble

and 'seven o'clock' he said severely, 'is late enough for anyone to be out...'. Marine surveyors usually have tales to tell, and the Hamble River practitioners were no exception. People who are wise make any offer for the purchase of a boat 'subject to survey' and get the craft vetted by the most reliable surveyor they know. There are two sides to this matter, of course. One very alert member of the profession turned down so many boats for one prospective buyer that the poor man went off at last and bought something without a survey. He remarked that he was getting on in years and despaired of ever getting afloat...

The surveyors have their problems too. One told a tale of a trip to Ireland. He was met by the owner of the little yard, the men who had built the boat, the priest who had blessed here when she was launched, and other interested parties. They assured him that a better boat never was built and that it was a waste of time to survey her. However, he stood firm, insisted that he had come all this way, and see her he must... and eventually did so. There was a lot of rot, so he summoned the boatyard owner, and digging his knife into the soft wood said, "Well, after all you told me, how do you account for this?" To which the man replied softly, "Sir, it must have been the fairies". Another said that the most frightening experience he ever had was when he was examining a steel Dutch yacht moored in a creek in some lonely marshes. His hammer went through one of the plates in the bow, and there he was, in the cramped fore part of the boat with water pouring in and no help within shouting distance. He must have felt rather like the little Dutch boy who put his finger in the hole in the dyke. Obviously the surveyor got out of the predicament somehow, but as he was extremely deaf, having suffered serious damage to his eardrums from gunfire while serving in the Navy during the war, it was very difficult to question him on any point, he carried on one-sided conversations without interruption.

The Officer in Charge of the Boom Defence operations was Captain Mansfield Smith Cumming R.N., who had an interesting conversion of an off-service floating bridge for his family living quarters, moored in the river off the pierhead. It was named 'Bridgewater House', and had been sold for £100 in 1896 after many years spent crossing the Itchen.

At the outbreak of the 1914/18 war Captain Cumming left 'Bridgewater House' to become "C" of the British Secret Service in London, and whilst on a mission to France, with his only son, Alastair, who was an officer in the Seaforth Highlanders, met with the most terrible accident, which was subsequently described in Sir Compton Mackenzie's book "Greek Memories". They were both pinned underneath their car when it overturned, and Captain Cumming hacked off his own smashed leg to get to his son to cover him with a coat. When they were eventually found Alastair was dead.

Captain Cumming returned and carried on his job in London for the rest of the war, and built 'Bursledon Lodge' (the later one) for his retirement, with the wonderful view down the estuary of the Hamble and across to the Island - he died quietly sitting in his chair in London before he could live there. He loved the river and the marshland, and was buried in Bursledon churchyard, near the War Memorial on which his son's name is recorded.

When 'Bridgewater House' began to leak just before the outbreak of the Second World War, it was put in on the marsh on the Sarisbury side of the river, but it eventually broke up, for when grounded such craft need a very flat site. A smaller floating bridge, towed from Barrow in Furness and also converted for Captain Cumming, was afloat in Bursledon Pool for some years as well.

Bearing in mind the size if these ferries, which are quite large, the drive-through portion made three good rooms, the central one having top lighting from dormer windows. The passenger accommodation around the vessel converted into sleeping cabins, bathrooms, etc. 'Bridgewater House' was owned in its latter years by Mr. Dan Hanbury of Castle Malwood in the New Forest. He and his family drove over to Bursledon in, what would now be,

priceless vintage Silver Ghost Rolls Royces, which were parked in Salterns Lane. The family were met and taken aboard by Bill Amor who kept the houseboat and its launches in spotless condition. That must have been the last of houseboating in the grand manner.

According to Mr. Harold Sims of Millbrook, who has delved into the history of the old ferries, the hull of 'Bridgewater House' was built by Hodgekinson of Crosshouse, Southampton, and conveyed the 'Red Rover' stagecoach (Bristol to Brighton) across the Itchen on its first journey in 1836.

There is the story, still remembered by many river folk, of the time a whale lost its bearings in the Upper Hamble. There was no call in those days (1932) to conserve wild life (and no census of endangered species) and so the whale was promptly shot.

The Upper Hamble valley is a splendid habitat for wild birds. The 'yaffle' of the green woodpecker is frequently heard and an occasional greater spotted woodpecker makes an appearance. There are blackbirds, thrushes, chaffinches, greenfinches, bullfinches, a few goldfinches, blue and coal tits, robins, sparrows, pigeons, owls and wrens, etc. A few years ago a hoopoe alighted in a garden at Sarisbury Court, and stayed a few days, causing much excitement amongst the birdwatching community. There are some jays and in the Bursledon and Hungerford area a great many of those glossy terrors, the strutting magpies. It would seem that these menaces to smaller birds have always been common to this neighbourhood, and nowadays are daily seen on the shoulders of the motorway along this stretch.

The Long Reach is a very pleasant part of the river because the banks are comparatively clear of buildings or development. On the west side - between Badnam Creek and Lands End Hard - there are the Salterns, creeks and sedges, which have been the natural aspect for hundreds of years. Here you find sea lavender, sea aster, gulls, terns, redshanks, curlews, and of course, the fishing cormorants and an inner ribbon of fields where cattle graze.

There have always been a few redshanks picking about between the boats in the mudberths in Bursledon Pool, cormorants fishing and spreading themselves to dry on posts, and, at Deacons, there was always one kingfisher flying from one mooring line to another, a gleam of blue - always just one - never more.

Before Moody's Marina was built, a pair of swans made a nest on the sedge each year, and each year it was wrecked by high tides. They never seemed to learn that it was a hopeless place, and everyone around suffered as much as the birds as they watched the water rising.

The short stretch of river between the A27 road bridge and the railway bridge has a boatyard on each bank. The one on the west bank was started originally by the Rev. George Kendall at the same time as he installed his daughters to run the Cabin Cafe. The Hamble River Boatyard opposite, on the east bank, began as a marine engineering business under the direction of a Mr. Arthur Cleaver in conjunction with Mr. Eddy Hamilton, (grandfather of the present "Echo" reporter, Keith Hamilton). It was subsequently owned by Mr. Reg Chalk for some years, and is now the base for R.K. Marine and Seasales U.K. The Spinnaker - their next door neighbour - was formerly the 'Red Lion', and in the field alongside, the Regatta Fair arrived and set up its roundabout, swings and bumper-cars etc. a few days before the actual regatta took place. For the remainder of the year it was used as grazing by the cows belonging to 'Nin', who herded them along what is now the A27 road, waving gaily to the few vehicles which then were driven by.

The fireworks have always been a great attraction at the end of this regatta - incidentally a splendid show of them cost £100, when the event was re-started after the 1939/45 war, and Mrs. Deacon always battled successfully for their retention when the members of the Committee showed signs of wavering at the ever-increasing cost... From the terrace of 'Upcott' there was a splendid view as they were let off from the point near Lands End Hard.

Just to the north of the railway bridge was a ford – in line with the old road to Winchester up which the pack animals plodded, now it is named Blundells Lane. The lovely old house here (somewhat obscured by a fence) is 'Maidenstone Heath', which was sold by a Mr. Blundell around the turn of the century to Captain Joshua Spencer-Smith who changed the name – rather appropriately – because he had eight daughters. The 'stone' part of it referred to a boulder which had come from a quarry at Warsash, and is said to be of glacial origin. There is a tantalising (and much too brief) reference to Mr. Blundell in Mr. W.W.Fox's notes. He says

"Grandfather Fox was paid £50 by Mr. Blundell of Blundell's Farm, now 'Maidenstone Heath', to substitute for him when conscripted to fight in the Napoleonic Wars".

Obviously Grandfather returned safely, if he did go to the wars, since he became bailiff to the Humphreys family at 'Elm Lodge' and subsequently brought up his family at 'Yew Trees'.

On the foreshore here is the boatyard of Foulkes & Son. The grandfather, Mr. J.R.Foulkes, and his wife and two sons, Alfred and Alwyn, arrived at Deacon's Yard in a sailing coaster in the nineteen twenties. They all worked there for some time, the sons in turn being Yard Bo'son. Alfred later went to Moody's Yard until his eventual retirement.

Alwyn raced very successfully in the old "Q" Class for Mr. J. Dudley Head, who was the 'father' of that Class in the Hamble. Alwyn was a born helmsman and boat handler. Unfortunately, he died at an early age, after starting his own yard, and it is his three sons, John, Bill and Glyn who carry on the business, After Mrs. Deacon's death in 1975, Bill bought 'Upcott', and lives there with his family, so the old house still has a connection with the river.

The Foulkes brothers now have a barge chandlery at Riverside yard and one beside the bridge on the A27 at Deacons Yard replacing the picturesque "Aladdin's Cave" which was their first treasure house for boat people.

On the east bank just north of the motorway bridge is a yard, 'Eastlands', which accommodates power craft, with road access off Swanwick Lane. Vessels with any height or fixed mast must remain below the A27 road bridge, so the upper reaches of the river are the province of motor boats and small sailing craft.

Brixedon Farm on the west bank just north of the motorway bridge is now a rather rare example of what a farm should be... There are cows and pigs, and the hens walk about the place freely, pecking as the fancy takes them. Mr. Game had farmed all his life but – very interestingly – was linked with the river through his mother who lived in the house at Hamble which is now the Royal Air Force Yacht Club, her family owning boats which went lobster fishing. Mr. Game lost land, and a good deal of tree shelter which his cattle needed, when the motorway was built.

*1960 Reggatta.
Alwyn Foulkes reassures
his grandson as Lightship Keeper*

*Bill and John Foukles (sons of Alwyn), outside
their original Aladdin's Cave at the Riverside Yard*

The farm is now on the edge of the Country Park which Hampshire County Council has made in the woods between here and Botley.

These woods, fifty years ago, were full of primroses, anenomes and bluebells, and were a delight to walkers and those who came by boat to picnic. During the 1939/45 war the Royal Marines' HMS "Cricket" was hidden in the woods, and their landing craft slipped in and out of the river on exercises until the invasion took place.

When the Marines left, the hutments were used for a time by homeless families, and were eventually demolished. To open up the Country Park a new road was made from Pylands Lane. Hampshire County Council's MANOR FARM at the Botley end of the Park has become a great attraction, particularly to children, who can see the animals in the yard of the old farmhouse, see how the family lived, and watch work in progress. At most weekends in the summer there are demonstrations of country crafts. The Farm is open from 10 a.m. to 5.30, or dusk, from Easter to October, and from October to Easter on Sundays only. The Park is open every day. There is a restaurant, and meals may be booked.One good thing to come out of the development to the north of Hoe Moor Creek was the establishment of the Queen Elizabeth Silver Jubilee Activity Centre, which was opened in 1978 by HRH Princess Margaret and has catered for many handicapped people of all ages who enjoy sailing, canoeing, camping etc.

The centre was honoured in 1983 by a visit from HRH The Princess of Wales, who expressed a wish to see the venture for herself. She arrived at Botley by helicopter on a very cold sunny December morning and was driven to the Centre, where the excitement was great. The Princess watched all the activities, saw the horse-riding group and travelled down through the woods to the river with some of the children in their special vehicle, to see the boats and their waterside sports. It was not a civic or pompous occasion: groups of local people and children waited under the trees to see the Princess pass by, but it was mainly a day for the disabled users of the Centre and their very special guest.

In the mud on the east bank lie buried remains of a vessel which, at the beginning of this century, was always referred to as the 'Viking Ship'. Souvenir hunters chipped off pieces of wood when low tides uncovered the hull. However, archaeologists were not convinced of the truth of this tale, and the late Mr. F.C.P. Naish, who then lived at 'Hamull' in Old Bursledon, and Mr. R.C. Anderson, established that the clinker built ship had been part of the fleet of Henry V; it was 125ft. long by more than 48ft. across the beam, which most exactly fitted the measurement of the "Grace Dieu". This vessel was moved to Bursledon in 1418 to lay up, and was burnt there in 1439, whether it caught fire or was struck by lightening in a storm is not known. However, when St. Leonard's Church at Bursledon put on a 'Son et Lumiere' in 1975 they took advantage of the doubt to include the effects of a great thunderstorm.

At the top end of this wooded reach is a little creek on the right, which can be negotiated by dinghy at high tide to Curbridge, which consists of a few old houses and the 'Horse and Jockey' inn.

Old Boathouse at Botley

Blundells Lane-the old road to Winchester

Fairthorne Manor built in 1854, extended in the 1880's, and purchased by the YMCA in 1947

The main part of the river continues on to Botley, but just ahead are the grounds of Fairthorne Manor, the YMCA National Training Centre, which caters for some 10,000 people each year, children and adults, out of work youngsters, and the handicapped. There are instructors skilled in sailing, canoeing, riding, archery, orienteering etc., A newly built Sports Hall is due to be opened by H.R.H. The Princess Royal. (1996). An appeal has been launched for £500,000 to build a new 115 bed dormitory block, as the present accommodation is very inadequate, and the house itself will only take a limited number of people. The brightly coloured canoes from Fairthorne Manor are a familiar sight all along the river, winter and summer. Some surprisingly large craft have emerged from the boatyard at Botley over the years, but of course they

A YMCA canoeing course on the upper reaches of the Hamble, in the 1950's

can only get out and down the river at high tide. In the old days, when boats were hired, it was always possible to tell from whence picnic parties had come, because the Botley boats were like Thames skiffs, with backrests, and slim lines, whereas the down-river people had more seagoing dinghies.

By the side of the road which crosses the river and ascends to Botley Square, is a stone commemorating William Cobbett, the 18th Century countryman who wrote "Rural Rides" and lived at Fairthorne Farm.

A few miles along this main road is the entrance to Botleigh Grange Hotel, an old house which Oliver Cromwell is said to have visited. In any event, there is a large picture of the Protector in the panelled dining room.

Richard St. Barbe Baker, the "Man of the Trees", was a great grandson of the Rev. Richard Baker, who was Rector of Botley for 51 years. The Rector died in 1854 at the age of 81 so he had seen many changes in the village, and the following notes were collected by the late Mrs. Phyllis Farwell from Richard St. Barbe Baker.

Botley old Church St Bartholomew

Up to 1798 all traffic – horse, carriage, coach, had to use the ford over the river by the mill – some travellers having to stay six hours in the village before being able to cross when the river was at high tide. This excerpt from a local guide shows how much Botley changed when the bridge was built:

Botley has but lately emerged from obscurity by the erection of a large brick bridge over the river, the fording of which was a traveller's curse and caused many people to prefer a long and circuitous route by Winchester. The river - which was formerly looked upon as its peculiar misfortune has become a source of riches and a scene of pleasure to its inhabitants.

The increase in traffic and communication brought a larger population, more houses were built round the Square and to the north of the village, and it became necessary to renew and enlarge the church accommodation.

This transfer must have entailed one of the most important changes in Richard Baker's career, and the designing and erecting of the parish church would have taken a good deal of thought. So from the little old 13th Century church of St. Bartholomew he came to be Rector of a modern church, All Saints, in 1836. Richard Baker was a country parson, fond of hunting, a good boxer, interested in farming the 800 acres of glebe land, and he spent £12.000 in planting trees. He was a farmer scholar and Fellow of Pembroke College, Cambridge, and when he exchanged his living in Norfolk for the one in Botley he drove the 200 miles in the family coach, changing horses en route. The coach was left in a paddock and became the home for generations of foraging (free range!) poultry.

His eldest son, Richard, also a scholar, coached his brother for Cambridge, and eventually went to Ontario. A younger brother, John, became a parson and had a living at Westend, he was the grandfather of the "Man of the Trees".

A Mrs. Emery was housekeeper for the Rector of Botley and retired at 83 to a cottage at Warsash provided by John Baker, where St. Barbe saw her when she was 103, with clear memories of happenings at the Old Rectory. The Rector encouraged the art of self defence in his parishioners, and often on Sunday afternoons a barrel of beer would be rolled out from the Rectory in support of a Botley champion who had taken on a challenger from Portsmouth. Baker himself was a good exponent of the art as two highwaymen found when they attacked the Rector on Lances Hill. He was returning from Southampton with the money to pay his labourers on the Glebe Farm. He tackled them both, with a little help from his mastiff, and marched them back to Southampton Bargate. He then walked the $8\frac{1}{2}$ miles home to Botley where (said his housekeeper) he turned up as fresh as a daisy... Mrs. Emery said there was blood on his cravat, but it certainly wasn't his.

He enjoyed his walking, and riding, and took his duties seriously, denouncing from the pulpit a certain local money-lender who had evicted poor widows from their cottages when they could not repay their indebtedness. He kept up a running battle with this man for some years, and also upset William Cobbett, the famous author of "Rural Rides", who lived nearby then at Steeple Court. Cobbett borrowed money from parishioners before he went to America, and on his return Parson Baker suggested it might be convenient for him to repay this, as in his absence one lady had been widowed and was in need of it. Cobbett was furious, at being told what to do, and from then on did all he could to avoid meeting the parson.

To mark the centenary of William Cobbett, Richard St. Barbe Baker organised a Cobbett Ride covering 330 miles in Hampshire, Surrey and Sussex, (actually linking two of the original rides together). He then invited all the Cobbett descendents he could find to lunch, with the Mayor of Southampton to entertain them. It was at this meal that one of the descendents told the story of a letter written by Cobbett which sent the Rector galloping off to London, only to find on arrival that the whole thing was a hoax. This get-together, and the fact that Richard St. Barbe Baker had talked to five schools a day on William Cobbett and Trees, made him feel that the feud had been truly laid to rest.

There was a mill at Botley for at least a thousand years, the present building being the third on roughly the same site; the two earlier ones being slightly upstream. It is one of the very few working mills still under private ownership, in this case the Appleby family, who also own one about one and a half miles northwards, along the river. The Open Days at the mill are extremely popular, and hundreds of people come to view the processes, and buy bags of flour, rolls and lardy cakes, to take home.

The central part as you enter has rough-hewn timbers which date back to the sixteenth century when the wooden ships for the Navy were constructed at Bursledon. Wickham Mill has similar timbers, and so do many of the local tithe barns. An interesting sidelight of the animal feed part of the business is that they supply specialised diets for the variety of animals at Marwell Wildlife Park. Following a serious fire in 1980 which destroyed the building where the animal feed was processed, this department has been transferred to a new site at West

End, hear the motorway, and other departments will follow over the next few years.

However, the mill will remain open as an historic building even though the growth of the business has made it necessary for a move. In particular, access for large lorries on and off the narrow A334 into the mill yard has been a serious problem in recent years. It is envisaged that in its new role the mill will continue to attract many visitors and become a feature of the Upper Hamble.

The Parish Church at Botley is beside the main road westwards from the Square, but Church Lane is out of the Square at the opposite end, St. Bartholomew's having been abandoned some years ago. The lane leads on past the Granary (now a sale room for a variety of household goods and 'surplus stock'), and by continuing straight ahead for about half a mile one finds the old church amongst trees, no longer awaiting little groups of parents with babies for christening, brides and grooms for weddings, or the slow approach of mourners. They have all gone. In 1981 the Church Commissioners gave notice of their intention to declare the church redundant and to appropriate it for use as a museum – this to be in association with the Country Park in the woods to the south.

Botley Mill marks the end of the tidal/navigational part of the river. Above the mill it is a leisurely stream which flows through the water meadows (with 'NO FISHING' notices), and under tiny bridges with white railings which carry the narrow winding lanes of the Durley area.
Durley is a scattered village, and the church is perched on a slight hill looking down upon the houses from a distance. There is a huge yew tree with an enormous trunk in the churchyard, and many of the gravestones date back to the sixteen hundreds. Gilbert White, the naturalist, was curate here before being appointed to Selbourne. No doubt he found quite a lot of interest in the Hamble valley too.

The largest industry here, apart from the farms is Houghton's Timber Yard, This has quite an interesting link with the river because in the days when the boat yards built wooden craft, dinghies and small yachts, there would be frequent journeys to Houghton's to find pieces of 'grown timber' which were naturally shaped to make, say, a curved stem or knee. A successful sortie of this kind, when a suitable piece was discovered, was sufficient to brighten any woodworker's day... There is no such fun with glass fibre construction!

The river can be traced northwards from Durley through meadows to the pond by the ruins of the Palace at Bishops Waltham, a pool fed by several brooks and runnels, and, in effect, the main source of the Hamble.

Bishops Waltham is a very ancient place, and the Palace or castle was founded by Henry de Blois (who ordered the Hamble monks to build the church at Bursledon). It was the favourite residence of William of Wykeham, and he died there in 1404, aged eighty. The bishops also owned a great park of about 1,000 acres around the palace.

St. Peter's, Bishops Waltham, is not the first church on this site. It is recorded that St. Boniface came here to be blessed in 715 before going to work in Germany among the heathen tribes, and in 1001 the Danes raided and burned the existing church and Waltham settlement. Incidentally, the present font is believed to be the original Saxon one; it was found in a rockery in 1933 and rededicated in 1965. The church handbook is

recommended for visitors wishing to sort out in their minds the process of rebuilding, which was begun by Henry de Blois, Bishop of Winchester, in 1136, and continued by William of Wykeham who died in 1404 at the Palace nearby, and work was continued through the years. The book also gives details of the eight bells, and various monuments, furnishings, etc. The clock came from the Palace after Cromwell's sacking in 1644. The memorial which has the most personal appeal is:

In memory of her beloved husband
THOMAS ASHTON
who after he had live 57 years providentlie
borne his sickness patientlie
disposed of his estate charitablie
ended his life Christianlie
lieth here interred decentlie
ANNE his desolate and disconsolate relict
hath erected this monument of his dissolution
7th August 1629
of her resolution to wayte all the days of her
appointed tyme untill her change shall come

The bust of Thomas Ashton is rather high on the wall, and a photograph has been placed below so that it can more readily be noticed, but it looks in remarkably good condition for something dating back to the reign of Charles I.

There are some beautiful flint walls in the surroundings of the church and vicarage, and Bishops Waltham is well worth a leisured visit of exploration. It strikes one as a very quiet place now, but according to chroniclers, it had sixteen public houses in days past, scenes of sport and merriment. French prisoners taken in the Napoleonic Wars were also housed in cellars, as the inhabitants did not know where to put them. but all appears to have ended happily, as they were given a farewell dinner on their eventual departure.

Henry II held a great council of nobles within the Palace walls in 1182 to raise money for his Crusade. Richard I was entertained there after his return from prison, and Margaret of Anjou was another visitor. The manor was sequestrated during the Civil War, and although it was returned to the see of Winchester at the Restoration, the building was no longer usable and the park was divided into farms. The ruins show the remains of a great hall, a chapel of the same dimensions, and a tower which was 17ft square.

There is a bypass round the little town now. Buildings worth noting are the Crown Hotel and Old Granary, which has been rehabilitated in recent years and is used as a restaurant and Craft Centre now. In years gone by local industries were iron casting and candle making, and according to the book "Paterson's Roads", published in 1824, there was a large trade in leather, the product being sent to *Guernsey and London and neighbouring fairs.*

One wonders if the leather for Guernsey was sent down the river and by way of the coasters lying off Bursledon. Bishops Waltham was included in the book because it was on a main road, whereas Hamble and Warsash, as we have seen, lead nowhere and so were not mentioned; Bursledon and Swanwick only had a brief note, their road and bridge being ready in about 1800, they just qualified for inclusion...

So this is a little of the history of the Hamble River – a waterway linked with a multitude of historic events and human lives reaching back into the past – and still the river flows strongly down past the woods and under the bridges and into the Solent, compulsively drawing to itself each new generation of our island people.

Wedding party at Bursledon Mill

Officer in charge of the Boom Defence. Capt. Mansfield S. Cumming, R.N. - pictured with the aeroplane in which he learnt to fly

The Toll Bridge with Deacon's Yard in foreground. Note the chimneys in background – the "Five Sisters" of Bursledon Brickworks.

Decon's Boatyard about 1950